CONTENTS

THE 1970s

People living in 1970s Britain saw a great many changes. The kind of money they used changed, the age at which young people were recognized as adults changed from 21 to 18, and because so many more women went out to work, there were changes in family life. Despite the gloom of rising prices and strikes, exciting new trends in entertainment and fashion made this a decade of great fun, particularly for the young. In this book, four people tell us what it was like to grow up in the seventies.

IAIN STEVENSON

Iain Stevenson was born in 1969 in south west London. In 1970 he and his family moved to Surrey.

▶ Iain in 1974 aged 5.

KATE JAMES

Kate James was born in 1965. She lived with her parents and older brother in an industrial town in South Wales.

▶ Kate in 1972 aged 7.

GRAEME WALKER

Graeme Walker was born in 1962 in Perth, Scotland. Throughout the seventies he and his younger sister lived in a small market town in Roxburghshire.

▶ Graeme in 1971 aged 9.

GHAZALA AHMED-MEAR

Ghazala Ahmed-Mear was born in 1963 in Lahore, Pakistan. She and her family moved to England when she was 9 months old. She lived with her parents and 3 brothers in Middlesex.

▶ Ghazala in 1973 aged 10.

Home life

By the mid-1970s the majority of households had labour-saving devices such as washing machines, and almost half had some kind of central heating, which meant that fires did not have to be laid every day. Housework was easier than ever before. Most homes had fridges and some had large freezers, so it was possible to buy most of the food shopping for a week in one trip.

Throughout the seventies there was an increasing number of large supermarkets all over the country.

Eating out

During the seventies, Chinese and Indian restaurants opened around Britain, some selling 'takeaway' meals. Fast food outlets selling pizza, hamburgers and other American-style food opened in the bigger towns and cities.

Iain

As a treat we used to get Chinese takeaways, which is still our favourite family meal. I remember one day I went to London with a group of older children, and we visited every fast food burger bar we could find to see which one was the best.

EATING IN

There was a great demand for 'convenience foods' that needed very little preparation. These could be frozen meals that just needed heating, or instant meals to which you simply added boiling water. At the same time books, magazines and TV programmes about cooking were very popular, and now that food from other countries was easier to buy, cooks could be adventurous.

VESTA Complete Dishes

Chow Mein with crispy noodles

This recipe contains dried ingredients, all keyed on back

Ghazala

We couldn't afford to eat out in those days. My mother cooked staple Pakistani food most days, and my dad even ate curry for breakfast. Occasionally on Saturday lunchtimes we had fish and chips or Kentucky Fried Chicken (we called this 'English dinner') but not without my dad putting lots of spices on his chips.

Seventies Fact

Up until the seventies it had been normal for a woman to be paid less than a man for doing the same job. During the 1970s two new laws were passed to help women get equality at work.

DECIMALIZATION

In 1970 Britain was using an old currency, or money, in which the pound was made up of 20 shillings, and a shilling was made up of 12 pennies. This all changed on 15 February 1971, when Britain adopted decimal currency. With 100 new pence to a pound, the new money was simpler and brought Britain in line with most of the rest of the world. Children quickly adapted but many older people found it hard to get used to the new money.

Old currency

New decimal currency

Kate

After decimalization I was very confused about my pocket money. I was used to getting a silver sixpence (a small coin worth 2.5 new pence) each week. It didn't seem right to be getting copper coins instead.

FUEL CRISIS

As a result of the Arab-Israeli War, in 1973 the price of oil from the Middle East quadrupled. Higher fuel costs, together with shortages caused by strikes, forced people to look for ways of saving energy.

DARK TIMES

Throughout the 1970s trade unions fought for higher wages through striking. The seven-week-long miners' strike of 1972 stopped the coal supply to power stations, which meant they could not produce electricity. There were frequent power cuts and the government introduced a three-day working week to conserve energy.

A post office using emergency lighting during a power cut.

Graeme

We were usually informed when there was to be a power cut and my mother would then plan a meal that she could cook on a camping stove because our cooker was electric. The nights when there was no electricity seemed very long and dark - and very cold. I remember going off to bed early, partly because there was nothing much to do and partly to keep warm.

School

Comprehensives

The change over to comprehensive schools that had started in the sixties, continued during the seventies. Under the old system children who failed the '11 Plus' exam went to secondary modern schools and those who passed went to grammar schools. The comprehensive system kept children together in the same school.

This purpose-built comprehensive school in Pimlico, London, opened in 1971.

Kate

I went to a church-run primary school for boys and girls and I was very happy there. After my '11 Plus' I went to a girls' grammar school. At first I was nervous and stuck close to the children I already knew from primary school but I soon got to like it there. Being girls only was wonderful and we never had to worry about what we looked like! When the school went co-educational in 1977 it felt strange to have boys in the building.

Iain

From age **5** to **11** I went to a small private 'prep' school for boys. I enjoyed all the sports we did - there were even judo and fencing classes after school. It was an old building and the headmaster was a very scary man. It was rumoured that if you misbehaved you got the cane but I only ever got the slipper.

Ghazala

The girls' grammar school was a handsome old building close to my home, and as a small child I always hoped I would go there one day. I passed my '11 Plus' so I did get to go and I loved it. I represented the school in sports events and enjoyed taking part in the school plays and helping to make the costumes. My school turned comprehensive while I was there and eventually closed after I finished fifth form, so I had to take my 'A' levels at a local college.

HAVING FUN

Now that so many households had stereo 'hi-fi' systems, cassette recorders, TV and, by the late seventies, video recorders, there was plenty of entertainment to be had in your own home.

Outside, there were youth clubs where young people could meet, and the ever-popular Girl Guides and Boy Scouts offered various activities, camping trips and the chance to learn practical skills. Discos organized and supervised by schools and youth clubs were something to get excited about.

◄ This VCR of the 1970s is bigger and less sophisticated than the ones we have today.

Kate

I was a member of a girls' choir during the seventies. We rehearsed at least twice a week and there were regular concerts and trips abroad. This picture shows us on tour in Canada.

Iain

I lived in a cul-de-sac which meant we could play in the street with the other kids without worrying about traffic. Sometimes we'd play cowboys and Indians, sometimes football, cricket or tennis. We spent a lot of time riding our bikes. My friend, who was a few years older than me, had a Chopper bike and I had the smaller version called a Chipper. We used to set up courses and have competitions on them.

13

TOYS AND GAMES

There was a series of 'crazes' for various toys and games during the seventies, encouraged by TV advertising. In 1970 the sophisticated Chopper bike went on sale, expensive at £32, but a dream machine of its day. In 1972 'Pong' was one of the first electronic games you could plug into your TV set. A game of on-screen table tennis, it was a great novelty then, but very basic by today's standards.

▲ Many toys of the time were 'spin-offs' from TV programmes or films, such as this game inspired by the hit movie *Jaws*.

Kate

One of my favourite toys of the time was a Spacehopper, a large ball for bouncing on with a grinning face and antennae to hold on to. I remember Klackers being a big playground craze - hard balls attached to elastic, which you swung to click together. They were actually quite dangerous.

Graeme

My sister had all the fashionable toys of the time - Spacehopper, pogo sticks, roller skates - but I wasn't into crazes. I had an Action Man though, and I used to save my money to buy 'Commando' books. They were small comics, about the size of paperback books, full of army stories.

Ghazala

I went to the occasional disco arranged by the school, but apart from that I was never really allowed to go out in the evenings. I learnt to knit when I was 6 years old and spent lots of time at home doing various needlecrafts and making clothes for my dolls.

THEN & NOW

• Top-selling toys of the 1970s included Lego and Action Man, both of which are still popular with children today.

15

FILMS

By the seventies 96 per cent of households had at least one television, and in 1973 the first video recorders went on sale. It was not surprising, therefore, that the number of people going to the cinema was dropping. However, there were some hugely successful films of the time. There were a number of 'disaster movies' about people fighting for survival against the odds, such as *The Poseidon Adventure* which was set inside a sinking ship.

The film *Jaws* (1975) about a killer shark had people on the edge of their seats.

Kate

Every Saturday morning I went to the local cinema which ran a special programme of cartoons for children. It was very popular and the cinema would always be full.

THEN & NOW

- In 1970 you could buy a cinema ticket for 6 shillings (30p). Now it costs around £4.50.

Graeme

*I remember going to see the film **The China Syndrome** in 1979, a thriller about a nuclear accident that almost ended in disaster. It was weird because just days after the film was released, it seemed to all come true when there was a similar accident at the Three Mile Island nuclear power station in the US.*

In *Saturday Night Fever* (1977), John Travolta's amazing disco dancing sparked a new dance craze. He also appeared in the musical *Grease* (1978) which was set in an American high school during the fifties. Music from both these films made number 1 hits in the record charts. 1977 was a good year for science fiction movies. *Close Encounters of the Third Kind* and *Star Wars* thrilled adults and children alike. Both films used dazzling special effects.

TELEVISION

During the seventies people were replacing their black and white televisions with colour sets. Programmes such as *The Magic Roundabout* made the most of bright and beautiful colours. It was a simple and funny animation with characters that included Dougal the dog, a kind girl called Florence, and a dozy rabbit called Dylan.

In contrast, the Saturday morning *Tiswas* show was a mad mixture of jokes, catchphrases, pop stars and slapstick. The 'Fantom Flan Flinger' threw custard pies around and 'prisoners' in The Cage were pelted with gooey stuff. American programmes, *The Banana Splits* and *The Muppet Show*, were big hits. *John Craven's Newsround* was the first news programme for children, and the realistic drama, *Grange Hill,* caused controversy with its storylines.

Authorised edition based on the popular Television series

Seventies Fact
In 1979 66 per cent of households had a colour TV and 31 per cent had black and white only.

Programmes for all the family included *The Morecambe and Wise Show* and *Dad's Army* — both of which are still shown today.

Ghazala

Ours was the first house in the street to have a colour TV - and with a 26-inch screen! Lots of neighbours dropped in on the Saturday it was delivered to have a look. I thought we were famous. As children we were only allowed to watch the BBC because my dad thought everything else was too trashy.

Graeme

I was a big fan of **The Magic Roundabout**, and Dougal was my favourite. There used to be free plastic models of the characters in our packets of breakfast cereal, and I used to fight with my sister over them. We liked watching **The Clangers** (pictured here), an animation about pink knitted mouse-like creatures from a blue planet that didn't talk but made whistling noises. I remember my mum making us Clangers out of old school socks and pipe cleaners which were really great.

THEN & NOW

- In 1971 a colour TV licence cost £12. Today it costs over £100.

FASHION AND MUSIC

With long hair, jeans and suits worn by both sexes, the early seventies was sometimes a time of 'unisex' fashion. For over half the decade trousers were flared, and got altogether wider when high-waisted 'Oxford bags' were in. Shoes and boots were high with sometimes enormous platform soles. For dressing up there was silver, suede, satin, crushed velvet and glitter.

Kate

I had a pair of red 'hot pants' in about 1972. These were short shorts with a bib at the front and were very fashionable for a while. Another favourite fashion item was my denim wedge shoes with embroidered flowers.

By 1976 hair was shorter, flared trousers finally went out of fashion and straight or tapered 'drainpipe' trousers came in. The most outrageous look of the time was 'punk' – spiky, coloured hair, and clothes with rips, zips, chains and lots of safety pins. Some of the girl 'punkettes' would wear black plastic bin liners or use old tin kettles as handbags.

Seventies Fact
To achieve a more shocking effect, some punks put safety pins through their cheeks, ears or through the skin just below the eyebrow.

Graeme
In the seventies we wore wide trousers, shirts with big collars and wide ties. When punk became fashionable I really admired it, but wasn't brave enough to dress like that. A boy at my school was the first punk in our town. I remember him ripping his school blazer, pinning it together with safety pins and pulling the sleeves half-off. He bleached his hair and coloured it green. I think he got sent home from school the next day.

POP MUSIC

Glamrock was the label given to the early seventies music of T-Rex, David Bowie, Slade, and many others. They all sounded different, but all wore glitzy clothes that were great fun. Two American family bands – The Osmonds and The Jackson Five – had followings among the under-16s, as did Scottish boy band The Bay City Rollers who started a new fashion with their tartan-trimmed denims.

After winning the Eurovision Song Contest in 1974, Swedish band Abba had many hit singles. Jamaican reggae music, typified by Bob Marley, was also around for most of the decade.

Vinyl records needed careful handling as they were easily damaged by scratches.

Ghazala

I was totally devoted to The Osmonds until 1975 when I discovered The Beatles. I was devastated to find they had split up in 1970. I even wrote down the words of their songs in a book.

NEW WAVE

In 1976 there was a completely different kind of music known as 'new wave', which was often harsh-sounding, rebellious and exciting. Its most extreme form was punk music which started with a band called The Sex Pistols, who shocked many with their songs, behaviour and appearance.

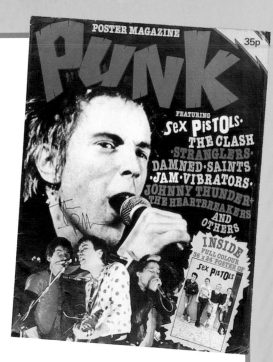

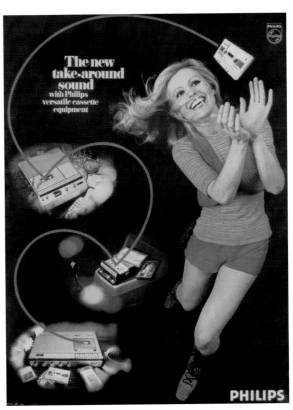

CASSETTES

Up until the early seventies music was only available on large vinyl records, but then along came neat cassette tapes and cassette players which made it easy to record whatever music you liked. In 1979 the smaller cassette players with headphones – 'personal stereos' – went on sale, so you could have music wherever you went.

Graeme

I used our cassette player to tape the record charts from Radio One on Sundays. I remember mucking around with my friends and taping ourselves through the microphone. We laughed so much at hearing each other's voices on tape.

TRAVELLING

Train travel became faster in 1976 when British Rail launched the new high-speed Inter-City 125 service. The number of families owning one or two cars continued to increase. Big selling models of the seventies included the Ford Cortina and the Ford Escort, while the Ford Capri, pictured below, was a popular sporty model. However, in the 1970s the British car industry was in decline and for the first time Britain was buying more imported new cars than British-made ones.

THEN & NOW

• In 1978 a Ford Escort could be bought for £2,328. In 2000 Ford stopped producing the Escort and replaced it with the Ford Focus which today can be bought for £10,495.

Iain

My dad had a succession of company cars which were Ford Granadas. Mum drove a Ford Cortina which was light blue and had plastic seats. It was a killer in the summer when I was taken to school in it wearing my shorts!

Graeme

We hardly ever went away on holidays, but we used to enjoy going off in the car for day trips. Sometimes friends or family would join us and we'd go in two cars. Here we are having a picnic on one of our trips.

AIR TRAVEL

In 1976 Concorde, the supersonic aircraft that travelled at twice the speed of sound, started making passenger flights. It was a very expensive way to travel, and very few could afford the fares.

Ghazala

Concorde used to pass over our house and we could always recognize it by its sound. We'd all rush out into the garden to watch it go over. At the time it seemed like something out of science fiction.

In 1970 the first Boeing 747 'Jumbo' service across the Atlantic began, carrying twice as many passengers as ordinary jet airliners. In 1977 Freddie Laker launched Skytrain, which offered tickets to New York for just £59 – less than a third of the usual price.

HOLIDAYS AT HOME

During the 1970s camping and caravan holidays were very popular with families taking their holidays in Britain. The British seaside continued to attract many holidaymakers.

Kate

We never went abroad but usually went to Devon or Dorset for our summer holiday. Dad said that he didn't trust an aeroplane to take us on holiday. We usually stayed in small hotels and visited places of historical interest.

On the beach at Margate, 1977.

HOLIDAYS ABROAD

With cheaper air fares available, an increasing number of holidays were taken overseas. The package holiday, providing accommodation, air travel and sometimes food at a set price, was something many found affordable. Popular destinations included Spain, Greece and Portugal.

Because of growing demand for package holidays, overdevelopment spoilt some of the more popular destinations.

Ghazala

In 1973 I went with my parents and baby brother on holiday to Pakistan for 4 weeks to visit our family. Flying was terribly exciting, but I didn't really enjoy being in Pakistan. It was extremely hot and the long train journey we made there was very uncomfortable.

Iain

We had one holiday abroad to Ibiza, which was very different then to how it is now. It was a package holiday and we stayed in a hotel. We didn't go abroad again because mum was scared of flying.

IN THE NEWS

THE SILVER JUBILEE

In June 1977 Britain celebrated the Queen's Silver Jubilee which marked 25 years of her reign. The Queen lit a bonfire at Windsor Park which was the signal for a line of bonfires to be lit across the country, and a week of celebrations followed.

Kate

There were street parties everywhere. The Queen visited our town and schoolchildren were allowed out to join people lining the streets to wave to her as she passed. My biggest thrill was singing in the choir that greeted the Queen during her visit, which was considered a great honour.

Street parties were held in cities, towns and villages all over Britain. The Queen travelled around the country meeting people.

Graeme

I remember all the street parties going on, but I didn't get involved in any of it. I was 15 years old at the time, into punk music and very anti-Royal.

BRITAIN JOINS EEC

On 1 January 1973 Britain joined the European Economic Community after great debate. The EU, as it is now known, was set up to make trade cheaper between European countries.

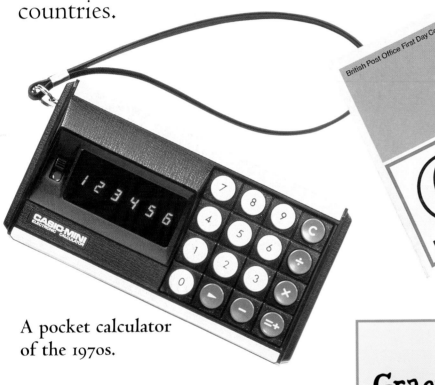

A pocket calculator of the 1970s.

POCKET CALCULATOR GOES ON SALE

In 1972 the first pocket calculator invented by Clive Sinclair went on sale. They were expensive at first, but got cheaper as time went by and more companies produced them.

Graeme

I remember the Sinclair pocket calculator causing a stir when it first came out. Children at our school were allowed to take them into class but not into exams. My parents thought it would ruin the ability to count so I didn't have one.

'THE KING' IS DEAD

'The King of Rock and Roll', Elvis Presley, was found dead in his Memphis home in August 1977. He had become a rock and roll idol in the 1950s. He died aged just 46.

Iain

*Although I was only **8** at the time, I can remember all the adults being in a state of shock when it was announced that Elvis was dead. I didn't know much about Elvis then, but I realized that he had been very important to many of my parents' generation.*

EUROPE'S FIRST WOMAN PRIME MINISTER

In 1979 Margaret Thatcher led the Conservative party to victory, when she was elected Britain's first woman prime minister. She remained in power until 1990.

Kate

*When Mrs Thatcher became prime minister in **1979**, my dad was shocked: 'What is the world coming to?' he said.*

FURTHER READING

Take Ten Years - *1970s*, Clint Twist, Evans Brothers, 1996

20th Century Fashion - *The 70s*, Sarah Gilmour, Heinemann, 2000

20th Century Music: *1970s - Years of Excess*, Jackie Gaff & Claire Oliver, Heinemann, 2002

When I Was Young - *The Seventies*, Neil Thomson, Franklin Watts, 1995

A Look at Life in the Seventies, RG Grant, Hodder Wayland, 2000

GLOSSARY

animation: When a series of drawings or photographs of puppets is filmed to create the impression that it has come to life.

conserving: Saving or protecting.

convenience food: Food that is sold ready or almost ready for eating.

cul-de-sac: A street that is closed off at one end.

decimalization: The introduction of a new system of money in 1971.

Eleven (11) Plus: An exam children sat aged 11 to decide which secondary school they would go on to.

European Union: Formerly known as the European Economic Community (EEC) and the European Community (EC), an association of European countries originally formed to improve trade between member nations.

overdevelopment: When a place has been spoilt by too many new buildings.

Oxford bags: Wide trousers with turn-ups.

power station: A place that generates electricity, often from burning coal.

punk rock: An aggressive style of pop music from the late seventies. Punk bands set out to shock with their lyrics and style of dressing.

shilling: An amount of money worth 12 old pennies (5p).

strike: When workers refuse to work because of a dispute, possibly over pay or working conditions.

supersonic: Faster than the speed of sound.

trade union: An association of workers of a particular trade or industry formed to protect their rights and wages.

unisex: A style of clothing worn by both men and women.

INDEX